Hey Love, Let's Journal Together

Hey L♡ve, Let's Journal Together

A LIGHTHEARTED MOTHER & DAUGHTER JOURNAL EXPERIENCE

Tawanna S. Cullen
Helaina J. Cullen
Fia S. Cullen

Disclaimer
The information in this book was correct at the time of publication, but the Authors do not assume any liability for loss or damage caused by errors or omissions.

©2022 by Tawanna Cullen, Helaina Cullen and Fia Cullen.

All Rights reserved. No part of this book may be reproduced or used in any manner without the prior written permission of the copyright owner.

Paperback ISBN 978-0-9837595-0-8
Hardback ISBN: 978-0-9837595-1-5

First paperback edition February 2022

Edited by Helaina Cullen and Fia Cullen
Cover art by Tawanna Cullen
Layout by Tawanna Cullen
Illustrations by Tawanna Cullen
Typeset in Alegreya Sans, Avenir, Barbieri, Beloved Sans, Chandler42, FatFrank-Heavy, Myriad Pro and Verdana

Printed by Kindle Direct Publishing in the USA

CelebrationBooksPublishing
An imprint of Celebration Books Publishing
Eastvale, CA 92880

tawannashantelle.com

This book is dedicated to you two.
It's dedicated to the devotion that you both have in getting to know each other and sharing such a special experience. We hope that you will create a keepsake out of this book and look back on it as time goes by. We hope that you continue on journaling together even after you finish this book. We hope that your mother/daughter relationship grows closer and stronger than ever. We hope that this journal will encourage you to share thoughts no matter how silly or serious they are. We hope that it will encourage you both to share ideas, opinions, dreams, and support each other.

This book is dedicated to
both of you.

This Journal Belongs To Us!

DRAW, DOODLE OR PASTE PICTURES ON THIS PAGE.

FAVORITE PHOTO OF US

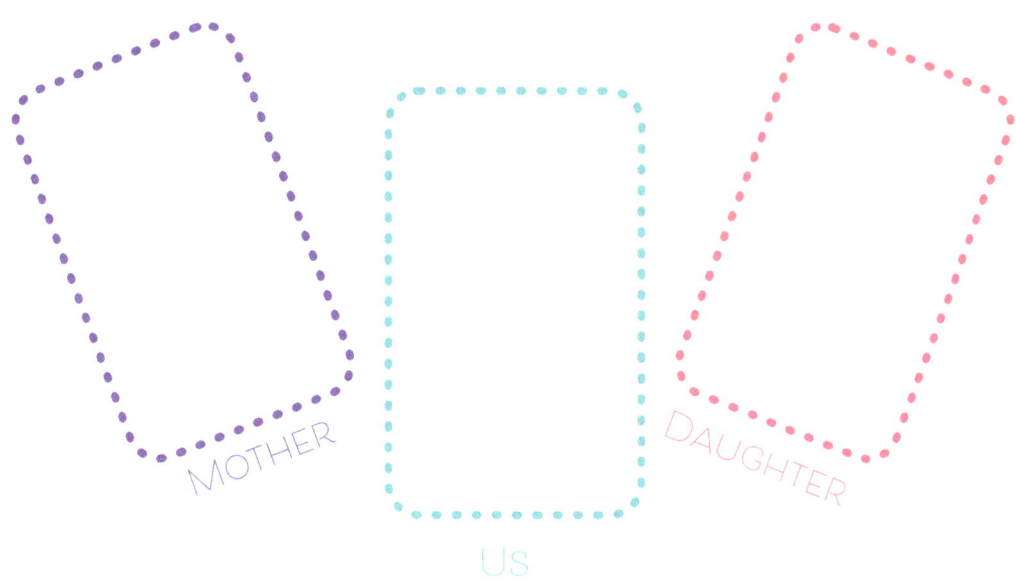

MOTHER

US

DAUGHTER

We started this journal together on:

Date: _____

A Note For Mothers:

I'm so excited you're journaling with your daughter! I hope this will be a fun and enlightening experience for both of you. Before you get started, I would like to share a few words of encouragement and maybe a little advice.

My daughters and I have enjoyed journaling together. I'm a mother of five kids who are different and unique in their very own special way. Helaina wrote out her answers faster than I expected, while Fia took her time. They set the pace for our journaling experience and it was a great, no pressure experience of journaling together. If your daughter isn't writing to you promptly it doesn't mean she isn't interested, she may not know the answers to some questions and may need a little more time to fill out the journal. Give her ample time to answer. This may be a day, two days, or maybe even weeks at a time. I was excited to fill out my portion and hand it to her, and even more excited to get to read her answers, however, some days I just had to wait.

If you are prone to correcting your daughter's spelling, try to refrain from grammar and spell checking in this journal. This could discourage her from writing to you. Could you imagine getting your journal back and it's been corrected like a homework assignment? That's not fun. This is a bonding journey for both of you, let the journal be a freedom space.

I would encourage conversations about the journal with your daughter because that allows you to get to enjoy each other more; however, I would be mindful of keeping the conversations private. This will build a bond of confidence and trust between you. What's said in the journal stays just between you and your daughter unless it's permissible with both of you to talk about some of the fun things in your journal in the company of others.

Before you start journaling, you'll both need to establish rules for your journaling experience. It is important that you do this together. Let her come up with some rules so this will be meaningful to her and she can take ownership in this experience as well. There are two pages to write down rules to establish the how, when, where, why and who of your journaling experience together. Honor the rules even if she doesn't. This is a great way to model how to honor and respect boundaries and it will establish trust between you.

This journal is meant to be mostly light-hearted but don't be surprised if there are a few entries that pull at your heartstrings. Take the opportunity to offer support to your daughter when she reveals things to you, or let her know you care. It will mean a lot for her to know you love her. I hope you enjoy this journaling experience and it becomes a personal bonding experience for you and your daughter.

Shantelle

A Note For Daughters:

We are so excited for you to do this journal with your mom! We've done a journal with our mom and we loved it, and we hope you enjoy spending time with your mom as much as we did with our mom! Here are a few things to know about this journal and some tips on how to use it!

Your writing doesn't have to be perfect! It's ok if you don't know how to spell a word, as long as you try your best!

Take your time. Everyone goes at their own pace. You don't have to complete it so quickly! You'll enjoy the experience more when you slow down and take time to think about what you are writing or doodling! Take as much time as you need!

Don't be picky about anyone's answers or doodles! If you pick at anything you don't like, then you might hurt your mom's feelings and the journal won't be as much fun. You get to answer the questions and doodle in your own way as much as your mom can too!

Keep your journal conversations between you and your mom! People don't like their business all out there. We limited our serious journal conversations to be just between us and our mom because we wanted to keep things private, but fun stuff we felt free to talk about.

Be Yourself! Don't put in answers that you think your mom would like or your friends would write! You do you! This is your mom and your journal! You write and doodle whatever you like or feel!

Encourage and support each other! This is supposed to be a fun and happy journal, but sometimes, things can be stressful in life so don't be afraid to write down some things you want to talk to your mom about! If your mom has something to say, listen, give her encouragement and support her in what she writes! This is about working together, learning about each other and giving each other advice. This is not just a book to write something in, it's your own personal journal, make it special!

Spend time and cherish each moment you have with your mom! This journal is also about spending time with each other and seeing your mom's point of view on things! You get to see your moms thoughts, feelings, and creativity shine through! Spending time with your mom can also make your relationship with her closer! So, enjoy each moment you have with her!

We hope that you enjoy this journal with your mom! Now that we've gone through some tips, here is how you use the journal...

Helaina & Fia

How to Use This Book

We are so excited you are journaling together! We hope this will be a fun and enlightening experience for both of you. Before you get started, here's some pointers on how to use this book.

This is a journal that you both will share. Mothers will write on one page and the daughters will write on the other page. You decide on how often and how many pages you want to fill out at one time. At the bottom of each page is a space to write the date, this is so when you look back at this book in the future you'll remember know when entries were written.

Mothers: When reading the questions, read them as if your daughter is asking you the questions, for instance, one of the questions asks, "What was it like when you were my age?" This would mean you would describe what life was like when you were your daughter's age.

Daughters: When reading the questions, read them like your mother is asking you the questions. Take time to answer the questions and be descriptive and write from your heart. The longer the answers the more your mother gets to know you!

This is a get to know each other book. Once you fill in the page(s), you hand it off to your mother or daughter. Read each others journal entrees and respond. It's really simple and fun to do. We suggest putting the journal in a designated spot so you know where to find it. We put ours by our bedsides.

The first step to getting started is to create your rules! Leave the rules page in the book so both of you can remember what you've agreed on. We suggest both of you make the rules so it's not just one person who is making the rules up. You both own this book and we hope it is something you will keep for a very long time and look back at in later years.

Lastly, Have fun!

Our Rules For Our Journal

This page lays out the rules for our journal. We have created these rules together and we both agree to them by signing below.

X _____ X _____
         (MOTHER)   (DAUGHTER)

X _____ X _____
     (MOTHER)   (DAUGHTER)

All About My Mother:

Name: ....

Preferred name or Nickname: ....

Birth date: .... Real Age: .... But I feel Like Age: ....

Height: .... Shoe Size: ....

Last Movie I watched:
....

If I could eat one food every day it would be:
....

Things I love: ....
....
....

My favorite Motto: ....
....

I want to do this journal with my Daughter because:
....
....
....

My favorite way to spend time with my Daughter is:
....
....

_____
Date:

All About My Daughter:

Name: ....

Preferred name or Nickname: ....

Birth date: .... Real Age: .... But I feel Like Age: ....

Height: .... Shoe Size: ....

Last Movie I watched:
....

If I could eat one food every day it would be:
....

Things I love: ....
....
....

My favorite Motto: ....
....

I want to do this journal with my Mother because:
....
....
....

My favorite way to spend time with my Mother is:
....
....

_____
Date:

Mother

My Top 3 Favorites!

My top 3 favorite songs

1.
2.
3.

My top 3 favorite movies

1.
2.
3.

My top 3 favorite books

1.
2.
3.

Date:

My Top 3 Favorites!

My top 3 favorite songs
1.
2.
3.

My top 3 favorite movies
1.
2.
3.

My top 3 favorite books
1.
2.
3.

Date:

Mother

My Top 3 UnFavorites!

My top 3 disliked songs

1.
2.
3.

My top 3 disliked movies

1.
2.
3.

My top 3 disliked books

1.
2.
3.

_____
Date:

My Top 3 UN Favorites!

My top 3 disliked songs

1.
2.
3.

My top 3 disliked movies

1.
2.
3.

My top 3 disliked books

1.
2.
3.

Date: _____

Mother

Why don't you like those songs?

....
....
....
....
....
....
....

Why don't you like those movies?

....
....
....
....
....
....
....

Why don't you like those books?

....
....
....
....
....
....
....

_____
Date:

Why don't you like those songs?

....
....
....
....
....
....
....

Why don't you like those movies?

....
....
....
....
....
....
....

Why don't you like those books?

....
....
....
....
....
....
....

Date:

Mother

What was your favorite school project or report about and what was it like to present it?

Date:

What are your favorite type of school projects or reports and how would you like to present them?

Date:

Mother

What's on your mind?

Date:

Daughter

WHAT'S ON YOUR MIND?

Date:

Mother

Doodle What your perfect house would look like outside.

Date:

DOODLE WHAT YOUR PERFECT HOUSE WOULD LOOK LIKE OUTSIDE.

Date:

Mother

My Favorite Things This Week

The best thing that happened this week:

....
....
....
....
....

My Favorite Products This Week:

....
....
....
....
....

My Favorite Everything Else This Week:

....
....
....
....
....
....
....

_____
Date:

My Favorite Things This Week

Daughter

The best thing that happened this week:

....
....
....
....
....

My Favorite Products This Week:

....
....
....
....
....

My Favorite Everything Else This Week:

....
....
....
....
....
....
....

Date: _____

Mother

Start writing a silly short story about a cat who thinks he or she is a giraffe with the best neck.

Date:

Conclude the silly short story your mother wrote about the cat who thinks he or she is a giraffe with the best neck.

Date:

Mother

My Top 3 Favorites!

My top 3 Countries I want to visit

1.
2.
3.

My top 3 TV shows

1.
2.
3.

My top 3 hobbies

1.
2.
3.

Date:

Daughter

My Top 3 Favorites!

My top 3 Countries I want to visit

1.
2.
3.

My top 3 TV shows

1.
2.
3.

My top 3 hobbies

1.
2.
3.

Date:

Mother

This OR That

Circle the one you prefer.

Fish Sandwich OR Chicken Sandwich?

Grey OR White?

Tacos OR Pizza?

Football OR Basketball?

Tennis OR Soccer?

Ballet OR Cheerleading?

Sketching OR Painting?

Running OR Walking?

Beach OR Mountains?

Reading OR Talking?

Skiing OR Ices Skating?

Flying A Kite OR Fishing?

Water Slide OR Regular Slide

Swings OR Jungle Gym

Caramel Apple OR S'mores?

Date: _____

THIS OR THAT

Circle the one you prefer.

Fish Sandwich OR Chicken Sandwich?
Grey OR White?
Tacos OR Pizza?
Football OR Basketball?
Tennis OR Soccer?
Ballet OR Cheerleading?
Sketching OR Painting?
Running OR Walking?
Beach OR Mountains?
Reading OR Talking?
Skiing OR Ices Skating?
Flying A Kite OR Fishing?
Water Slide OR Regular Slide
Swings OR Jungle Gym
Caramel Apple OR S'mores?

Date: _____

Mother

Ask Me 3 Questions:

Daughter's Question 1:
....
....

Mother's Answer:
....
....
....

Daughter's Question 2:
....
....

Mother's Answer:
....
....
....

Daughter's Question 3:
....
....

Mother"s Answer:
....
....
....

_____
Date:

Ask Me 3 Questions:  Daughter

Mother's Question 1:

....

....

Daughter's Answer:

....

....

....

Mother's Question 2:

....

....

Daughter's Answer:

....

....

....

Mother's Question 3:

....

....

Daughter's Answer:

....

....

....

_____

Date:

Mother

How old will you be in 5 years and where do you want to be in 5 years?

Date:

How old will you be in 5 years and where do you want to be in 5 years?

Date:

Mother

My Favorite Things This Week

The Best Thing That Happened This Week:

My Favorite Products This Week:

My Favorite Everything Else This Week:

Date:

My Favorite Things This Week

 Daughter

The best thing that happened this week:

....
....
....
....
....

My Favorite Products This Week:

....
....
....
....
....

My Favorite Everything Else This Week:

....
....
....
....
....
....
....

_____
Date:

Mother

DOODLE WHAT YOUR PERFECT OUTFIT ON THE RED CARPET OR A FORMAL EVENT WOULD LOOK LIKE.

DOODLE WHAT YOUR DAUGHTER'S PERFECT OUTFIT ON THE RED CARPET OR A FORMAL EVENT WOULD LOOK LIKE.

Date:

 **Daughter**

Doodle What your perfect outfit on the red carpet or a formal event would look like.

Doodle What your Mother's perfect outfit on the red carpet or a formal event would look like.

Date:

My Ultimate Life Bucket List

List below the things you would love to do.

_____

_____

_____

_____

_____

_____

_____

_____

_____

_____

_____

_____

_____

_____

_____

Date:

My Ultimate Life Bucket List

List below the things you would love to do.

Date: _____

Mother

5 Quick Questions

Favorite toy growing up:

Favorite color as a kid:

Least liked color as a kid:

Favorite sport growing up:

Favorite restaurant as a kid:

Date:

5 Quick Questions

Daughter

Favorite toy when I was 5:

Favorite color when I was 5:

Least liked color when I was 5:

Favorite sport when I was 5:

Favorite restaurant when I was 5:

Date:

Mother

These are my biggest fears and why:

Date:

These are my biggest fears and why:

Date:

Mother

My Top 3 UN Favorites!

My top 3 Places I never want to go.

1.
2.
3.

My top 3 Disliked TV Shows

1.
2.
3.

My top 3 disliked Activities

1.
2.
3.

Date:

 **Daughter**

My Top 3 UN Favorites!

My top 3 Places I never want to go.

1.
2.
3.

My top 3 Disliked TV Shows

1.
2.
3.

My top 3 disliked Activities

1.
2.
3.

Date: _____

Mother

Why don't you like those places?

....
....
....
....
....
....
....

Why don't you like those TV Shows?

....
....
....
....
....
....
....

Why don't you like those activities?

....
....
....
....
....
....
....

Date:

Daughter

Why don't you like those places?

_____
_____
_____
_____
_____
_____
_____

Why don't you like those TV Shows?

_____
_____
_____
_____
_____
_____
_____

Why don't you like those activities?

_____
_____
_____
_____
_____
_____
_____

Date:

Mother

What's on your mind?

_____
Date:

WHAT'S ON YOUR MIND?

....
....
....
....
....
....
....
....
....
....
....
....
....
....
....
....
....
....

_____
Date:

Mother

If you could appear in any story book, which one would you pick and what would you do?

Date:

If you could appear in any story book, which one would you pick and what would you do?

Date:

Mother

My Favorite Things This Week

The best thing that happened this week:

....
....
....
....
....

My Favorite Products This Week:

....
....
....
....

My Favorite Everything Else This Week:

....
....
....
....
....
....
....

_____
Date:

My Favorite Things This Week

 Daughter

The best thing that happened this week:

....
....
....
....
....

My Favorite Products This Week:

....
....
....
....
....

My Favorite Everything Else This Week:

....
....
....
....
....
....
....

_____
Date:

Mother

DOODLE WHAT YOUR IMAGINARY PET WOULD LOOK LIKE.

Date:

DOODLE WHAT YOUR IMAGINARY PET WOULD LOOK LIKE.

Date:

Circle the one you prefer.

1. Do you want pets? YES NO

2. Have you traveled outside of the country? YES NO

3. Can you do a cartwheel? YES NO

4. Do you like to run? YES NO

5. Do you like to wear dresses? YES NO

6. Do you like to sushi? YES NO

7. Have you been to a drive-in theater? YES NO

8. Do you like Roller Coasters? YES NO

9. Do you like doing science experiments? YES NO

10. Can you curl your tongue? YES NO

Date:

Mother

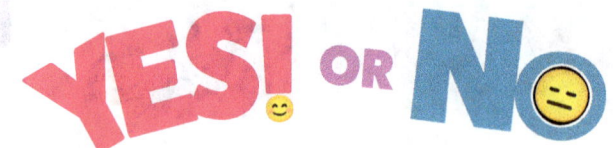

CIRCLE THE ONE YOU PREFER.

1. Did you have pets growing up? YES NO

2. Have you traveled outside of the country? YES NO

3. Can you do a cartwheel? YES NO

4. Do you like to run? YES NO

5. Do you like to wear dresses? YES NO

6. Do you like to sushi? YES NO

7. Have you been to a drive-in theater? YES NO

8. Do you like roller coasters? YES NO

9. Do you like doing science experiments? YES NO

10. Can you curl your tongue? YES NO

Date:

Mother

This or That

Circle the one you prefer.

Ponytail OR Hair Down

Short Hair OR Long Hair

Shorts OR Pants

Dress OR Pants

Reading OR Being Read To

Movies OR Tv Shows

Milk Shake OR Ice Cream Cone

Cats OR Dogs

City OR Country

Singing OR Dancing

Cartwheels OR Jumping Jacks

Lemonade OR Ice Tea

Yoga OR Tai Chi

Shopping OR Save Money

Pancakes OR Waffles

Date:

THIS OR THAT

Circle the one you prefer.

Ponytail	OR	Hair Down
Short Hair	OR	Long Hair
Shorts	OR	Pants
Dress	OR	Pants
Reading	OR	Being Read To
Movies	OR	Tv Shows
Milk Shake	OR	Ice Cream Cone
Cats	OR	Dogs
City	OR	Country
Singing	OR	Dancing
Cartwheels	OR	Jumping Jacks
Lemonade	OR	Ice Tea
Yoga	OR	Tai Chi
Shopping	OR	Save Money
Pancakes	OR	Waffles

Date: _____

Mother

What was your most embarrassing moment?

Date:

What was you most embarrassing moment?

Date:

Mother

Ask Me 3 Questions:

Daughter's Question 1:

....

....

Mother's Answer:

....

....

....

Daughter's Question 2:

....

....

Mother's Answer:

....

....

....

Daughter's Question 3:

....

....

Mother"s Answer:

....

....

....

_____
Date:

Ask Me 3 Questions:

Mother's Question 1:
....
....

Daughter's Answer:
....
....
....

Mother's Question 2:
....
....

Daughter's Answer:
....
....
....

Mother's Question 3:
....
....

Daughter's Answer:
....
....
....

_____
Date:

My Top 3 Favorites!

My top 3 Board Games

1.
2.
3.

My top 3 Favorite Stores

1.
2.
3.

My top 3 Favorite Sports

1.
2.
3.

Date:

Daughter

My Top 3 Favorites!

My top 3 Board Games
1.
2.
3.

My top 3 Favorite Stores
1.
2.
3.

My top 3 Favorite Sports
1.
2.
3.

Date: _____

Mother

If you could relive a day or moment in your life, which would it be and why?

Date:

If you could relive a day or moment in your life, which would it be and why?

Date:

Mother

My Favorite Things This Week

The best thing that happened this week:

....
....
....
....
....

My Favorite Products This Week:

....
....
....
....
....

My Favorite Everything Else This Week:

....
....
....
....
....
....
....

Date:

My Favorite Things This Week

The best thing that happened this week:

....
....
....
....
....

My Favorite Products This Week:

....
....
....
....

My Favorite Everything Else This Week:

....
....
....
....
....
....
....

_____
Date:

Mother

CREATE A MAZE FOR YOUR DAUGHTER TO SOLVE.

Date:

Daughter

CREATE A MAZE FOR YOUR MOTHER TO SOLVE.

Date:

Mother

5 Quick Questions

What is your favorite dish to eat?

Where is your favorite place to read?

What is your favorite shirt?

What is your favorite quote, scripture or saying?

What is your favorite radio station?

Date:

5 Quick Questions

Daughter

What is your favorite dish to eat?

Where is your favorite place to read?

What is your favorite shirt?

What is your favorite quote, scripture or saying?

What is your favorite radio station?

Date:

Mother

What was the strangest dream you've ever had?

Date:

Daughter

What was the strangest dream you've ever had?

Date:

Mother

THIS OR THAT

Circle the one you prefer.

Calling OR Texting

Cooking Dinner OR Baking Dessert

Cook At Home OR Eat Out

Sweet OR Sour

Sunny Days OR Rainy Days

Laptop OR Tablet

Bears OR Bunnies

Travel By Plane OR Travel By Train

Scary Movies OR Funny Movies

Action OR Comedy

Sneakers OR Sandals

Outer Space OR Deep Ocean

Simple OR Glam

Tokyo OR Paris

Strawberries OR Blueberries

_____
Date:

THIS OR THAT

Circle the one you prefer.

Calling	OR	Texting
Cooking Dinner	OR	Baking Dessert
Cook At Home	OR	Eat Out
Sweet	OR	Sour
Sunny Days	OR	Rainy Days
Laptop	OR	Tablet
Bears	OR	Bunnies
Travel By Plane	OR	Travel By Train
Scary Movies	OR	Funny Movies
Action	OR	Comedy
Sneakers	OR	Sandals
Outer Space	OR	Deep Ocean
Simple	OR	Glam
Tokyo	OR	Paris
Strawberries	OR	Blueberries

Date: _____

Mother

If you could draw anything that would become real, what would you draw and what would it do?

Date:

Daughter

If you could draw anything that would become real, what would you draw and what would it do?

Date:

Mother

Would You Rather

Circle the one you prefer.

Would you rather be a superhero in a movie or
Would you rather be a villain in a movie?

Would you rather be invisible or
Would you rather be able to fly?

Would you rather always be formally dressed or
Would you rather always be causally dressed?

Would you rather be famous and rich or
Would you rather be unknown and rich?

Would you rather discover a new planet or
Would you rather discover a new sea creature?

Would you rather live in a tree house or
Would you rather live in a house on the sea?

Would you rather fight in a zombie apocalypse or
Would you rather fight in a robot apocalypse?

Date:

Would You Rather

Daughter

Circle the one you prefer.

Would you rather be a superhero in a movie or
Would you rather be a villain in a movie?

Would you rather be invisible or
Would you rather be able to fly?

Would you rather always be formally dressed or
Would you rather always be causally dressed?

Would you rather be famous and rich or
Would you rather be unknown and rich?

Would you rather discover a new planet or
Would you rather discover a new sea creature?

Would you rather live in a tree house or
Would you rather live in a house on the sea?

Would you rather fight in a zombie apocalypse or
Would you rather fight in a robot apocalypse?

_____
Date:

Mother

WHAT'S ON YOUR MIND?

Date:

Daughter

WHAT'S ON YOUR MIND?

Date: _____

Mother

My Favorite Things This Week

The best thing that happened this week:

....
....
....
....
....

My Favorite Products This Week:

....
....
....
....
....

My Favorite Everything Else This Week:

....
....
....
....
....
....
....

_____
Date:

My Favorite Things This Week

Daughter

The best thing that happened this week:

....
....
....
....
....

My Favorite Products This Week:

....
....
....
....
....

My Favorite Everything Else This Week:

....
....
....
....
....
....
....

_____
Date:

Mother

Ask Me 3 Questions:

Daughter's Question 1:
_____
_____

Mother's Answer:
_____
_____
_____

Daughter's Question 2:
_____
_____

Mother's Answer:
_____
_____
_____

Daughter's Question 3:
_____
_____

Mother"s Answer:
_____
_____
_____

_____
Date:

Ask Me 3 Questions: Daughter

Mother's Question 1:

Daughter's Answer:

Mother's Question 2:

Daughter's Answer:

Mother's Question 3:

Daughter's Answer:

Date:

Mother

What historical person would you want to spend the day with? Describe a perfect day with them.

Date:

What historical person would you want to spend the day with? Describe a perfect day with them.

Date:

Mother

DOODLE LOTS OF YOUR FAVORITE SHAPES.

Date:

DOODLE LOTS OF YOUR FAVORITE SHAPES.

Date:

Mother

My Top 3 UN Favorites!

My top 3 disliked games

1.
2.
3.

My top 3 disliked stores

1.
2.
3.

My top 3 disliked sports

1.
2.
3.

Date:

My Top 3 UN Favorites!

My top 3 disliked games
1.
2.
3.

My top 3 disliked stores
1.
2.
3.

My top 3 disliked sports
1.
2.
3.

Date: _____

Mother

Why don't you like those games?

_____
_____
_____
_____
_____
_____
_____
_____

Why don't you like those stores?

_____
_____
_____
_____
_____
_____
_____
_____

Why don't you like those sports?

_____
_____
_____
_____
_____
_____
_____
_____

_____
Date:

Daughter

WHY DON'T YOU LIKE THOSE GAMES?

....
....
....
....
....
....
....
....

WHY DON'T YOU LIKE THOSE STORES?

....
....
....
....
....
....
....
....

WHY DON'T YOU LIKE THOSE SPORTS?

....
....
....
....
....
....
....
....

Date: _____

Mother

If you could assign each person in your family superpowers, who would get what power and why?

Date:

Daughter

If you could assign each person in your family superpowers, who would get what power and why?

Date:

Mother

5 Quick Questions

1. What is/was your favorite subject in school?

   ----

2. What is your favorite chip flavor?

   ----

3. What is your favorite dance move?

   ----

4. What is your favorite magazine?

   ----

5. Who would you swap lives with for 24 hours?

_____
Date:

5 Quick Questions

Daughter

What is your favorite subject in school?

What is your favorite chip flavor?

What is your favorite dance move?

What is your favorite magazine?

Who would you swap lives with for 24 hours?

Date:

Mother

My Favorite Things This Week

The Best Thing That Happened This Week:

....
....
....
....
....

My Favorite Products This Week:

....
....
....
....

My Favorite Everything Else This Week:

....
....
....
....
....
....

_____
Date:

My Favorite Things This Week

The Best Thing That Happened This Week:

....
....
....
....
....

My Favorite Products This Week:

....
....
....
....
....

My Favorite Everything Else This Week:

....
....
....
....
....
....
....

_____
Date:

Mother

DOODLE CUTE BUGS.

Date:

Daughter

DOODLE CUTE BUGS.

Date:

Mother

Ask Me 3 Questions:

Daughter's Question 1:
....
....

Mother's Answer:
....
....
....

Daughter's Question 2:
....
....

Mother's Answer:
....
....
....

Daughter's Question 3:
....
....

Mother"s Answer:
....
....
....

_____
Date:

Ask Me 3 Questions: **Daughter**

Mother's Question 1:

....

....

Daughter's Answer:

....

....

....

Mother's Question 2:

....

....

Daughter's Answer:

....

....

....

Mother's Question 3:

....

....

Daughter's Answer:

....

....

....

_____
Date:

Mother

Describe your perfect vacation.

Date:

Daughter

Describe your perfect vacation.

Date:

Mother

My Top 3 Favorites!

My top 3 Favorite Candies

1.
2.
3.

My top 3 Favorite Animals

1.
2.
3.

My top 3 Favorite Beverages

1.
2.
3.

_____
Date:

My Top 3 Favorites!

My top 3 Favorite Candies

1.
2.
3.

My top 3 Favorite Animals

1.
2.
3.

My top 3 Favorite Beverages

1.
2.
3.

Date: _____

Mother

 OR

Circle the one you prefer.

1. Have you ever thought about changing your name?   YES   NO

2. Have you cried while watching a movie?   YES   NO

3. Can you sew?   YES   NO

4. If you found a wallet of money would you return it?   YES   NO

5. Have you ever been fishing?   YES   NO

6. Do you like flying kites?   YES   NO

7. Do you like making s'mores?   YES   NO

8. Have you ever been ice skating?   YES   NO

9. Have you ever picked apples off of a tree?   YES   NO

10. Do you like water slides?   YES   NO

_____
Date:

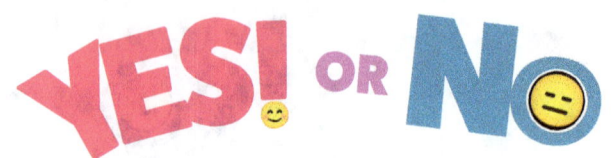 

Circle the one you prefer.

1. Have you ever thought about changing your name?   YES   NO

2. Have you cried while watching a movie?   YES   NO

3. Can you sew?   YES   NO

4. If you found a wallet of money would you return it?   YES   NO

5. Have you ever been fishing?   YES   NO

6. Do you like flying kites?   YES   NO

7. Do you like making s'mores?   YES   NO

8. Have you ever been ice skating?   YES   NO

9. Have you ever picked apples off of a tree?   YES   NO

10. Do you like water slides?   YES   NO

_____
Date:

Mother

What's on your mind?

_____

_____

_____

_____

_____

_____

_____

_____

_____

_____

_____

_____

_____

_____

_____

_____

_____

_____

Date: _____

What's on your mind?

Date:

Mother

If you could time travel, where would you go and what time period would you go to?

Date:

Daughter

If you could time travel, where would you go and what time period would you go to?

Date:

Mother

My Favorite Things This Week

The best thing that happened this week:

....
....
....
....
....

My Favorite Products This Week:

....
....
....
....
....

My Favorite Everything Else This Week:

....
....
....
....
....
....
....

Date:

My Favorite Things This Week

The Best Thing That Happened This Week:

....

....

....

....

....

My Favorite Products This Week:

....

....

....

....

....

My Favorite Everything Else This Week:

....

....

....

....

....

....

....

Date: _____

Mother

DOODLE YOUR FAVORITE PATTERNS.

Date:

DOODLE YOUR FAVORITE PATTERNS.

Date:

Mother

5 Quick Questions

Who inspires you?

Would you trade looks for intelligence or intelligence for looks?

If you had a warning label what would it say?

Would you be the worst player on the best team or the best player on the worst team?

If you joined the circus, what would you do?

Date:

5 Quick Questions

Daughter

Who inspires you?

....

Would you trade some looks for intelligence or intelligence for looks?

....

If you had a warning label what would it say?

....

Would you be the worst player on the best team or the best player on the worst team?

....

If you joined the circus, what would you do?

....

Date:

Mother

What do you think your Daughter's best qualities are?

Date:

What do you think your Mother's best qualities are?

Date:

Mother

My Top 3 Favorites!

TOP 3 FAVORITE CARS

1.
2.
3.

TOP 3 Favorite Celebrities

1.
2.
3.

My top 3 Favorite Flowers

1.
2.
3.

_____
Date:

My Top 3 Favorites!

TOP 3 FAVORITE CARS

1.
2.
3.

TOP 3 Favorite Celebrities

1.
2.
3.

My top 3 Favorite Flowers

1.
2.
3.

Date: _____

Mother

Would You Rather

Circle the one you prefer.

Would you rather sneeze constantly or
Would you rather drool constantly?

Would you rather have a robot clean your house daily or
Would you rather have a robot cook your food daily?

Would you rather only respond with emojis or
would you rather only respond with gifs?

Would you rather be stuck snowed in the mountains or
Would you rather be stuck in a heatwave in the desert?

Would you rather be in a world wide sing off with a horse voice or
would you rather be in a world wide dance off with a broken leg?

Would you rather run at 110 miles per hour or
Would you rather fly at 25 miles per hour?

Would you rather be stuck in a food fight or
would you rather be stuck in a water balloon fight?

Date:

Would You Rather

Daughter

Circle the one you prefer.

Would you rather sneeze constantly or
Would you rather drool constantly?

Would you rather have a robot clean your house daily or
Would you rather have a robot cook your food daily?

Would you rather only respond with emojis or
Would you rather only respond with gifs?

Would you rather be stuck snowed in the mountains or
Would you rather be stuck in a heatwave in the desert?

Would you rather be in a world wide sing off with a horse voice or
Would you rather be in a world wide dance off with a broken leg?

Would you rather run at 110 miles per hour or
Would you rather fly at 25 miles per hour?

Would you rather be stuck in a food fight or
Would you rather be stuck in a water balloon fight?

Date: _____

Mother

Doodle flowers and plants.

Date:

DOODLE FLOWERS AND PLANTS.

Date:

Mother

My Favorite Things This Week

The Best Thing That Happened This Week:

....
....
....
....
....

My Favorite Products This Week:

....
....
....
....
....

My Favorite Everything Else This Week:

....
....
....
....
....
....
....

_____
Date:

My Favorite Things This Week

 **Daughter**

The best thing that happened this week:

....
....
....
....
....

My Favorite Products This Week:

....
....
....
....
....

My Favorite Everything Else This Week:

....
....
....
....
....
....
....

_____
Date:

Mother

What was life like when you were your Daughter's age?

Date:

What do you think life will be like when you are your Mother's age?

Date:

Mother

My Top 3 UN Favorites!

My top 3 disliked bugs

1.
2.
3.

My top 3 disliked fruits or veggies

1.
2.
3.

My top 3 disliked subjects

1.
2.
3.

Date:

Daughter

My Top 3 UN Favorites!

My top 3 disliked bugs
1.
2.
3.

My top 3 disliked fruits or veggies
1.
2.
3.

My top 3 disliked subjects
1.
2.
3.

Date: _____

Mother

Why don't you like those bugs?

Why don't you like those fruits or veggies?

Why don't you like those subjects?

Date:

Daughter

Why don't you like those bugs?

_____
_____
_____
_____
_____
_____
_____

Why don't you like those fruits or veggies?

_____
_____
_____
_____
_____
_____
_____

Why don't you like those subjects?

_____
_____
_____
_____
_____
_____
_____

Date:

Mother

Ask Me 3 Questions:

Daughter's Question 1:
....
....

Mother's Answer:
....
....
....

Daughter's Question 2:
....
....

Mother's Answer:
....
....
....

Daughter's Question 3:
....
....

Mother"s Answer:
....
....
....

Date:

Ask Me 3 Questions: **Daughter**

Mother's Question 1:
....
....

Daughter's Answer:
....
....
....

Mother's Question 2:
....
....

Daughter's Answer:
....
....
....

Mother's Question 3:
....
....

Daughter's Answer:
....
....
....

_____
Date:

Mother

What are 5 things about your Daughter that make you smile?

Date:

Daughter

What are 5 things about your Mother that make you smile?

Date:

Mother

Circle the one you prefer.

1. Do you like staying in hotels?   YES   NO

2. Have you ever been camping?   YES   NO

3. Do you like camping?   YES   NO

4. Do you like spicy food?   YES   NO

5. Have you ever met someone famous?   YES   NO

6. Are you a thrill seeker?   YES   NO

7. Do spiders scare you?   YES   NO

8. Have you ever been bullied?   YES   NO

9. Have you ever cheated on a test?   YES   NO

10. Have you ever stood up for a friend?   YES   NO

Date:

CIRCLE THE ONE YOU PREFER.

1. Do you like staying in hotels?   YES   NO

2. Have you ever been camping?   YES   NO

3. Do you like camping?   YES   NO

4. Do you like spicy food?   YES   NO

5. Have you ever met someone famous?   YES   NO

6. Are you a thrill seeker?   YES   NO

7. Do spiders scare you?   YES   NO

8. Have you ever been bullied?   YES   NO

9. Have you ever cheated on a test?   YES   NO

10. Have you ever stood up for a friend?   YES   NO

Date: _____

DOODLE SPACE THINGS.

Date:

Daughter

DOODLE SPACE THINGS.

Date:

Mother

My Favorite Things This Week

The Best Thing That Happened This Week:

....
....
....
....
....

My Favorite Products This Week:

....
....
....
....
....

My Favorite Everything Else This Week:

....
....
....
....
....
....
....

_____
Date:

My Favorite Things This Week

 Daughter

The best thing that happened this week:

....
....
....
....
....

My Favorite Products This Week:

....
....
....
....
....

My Favorite Everything Else This Week:

....
....
....
....
....
....
....

_____
Date:

Mother

What can your Daughter do to be the best person she can be?

Date:

What can your Mother do to be the best person she can be?

Date:

THIS OR THAT

Circle the one you prefer.

Cartoons	OR	Live Action
Art	OR	Math
Plan It	OR	Wing It
Backpack	OR	Suitcase
Early Bird	OR	Night Owl
Sunrise	OR	Sunset
Dreamer	OR	Realist
Always Early	OR	Always Late
Vanilla	OR	Chocolate
Talk To All Animals	OR	Speak All Languages
Be Invisible	OR	Fly
Socks	OR	Bare Feet
Sun	OR	Moon
Ice Cream	OR	Gelato
Hot Dog	OR	Hamburger

Date:

THIS OR THAT

Daughter

CIRCLE THE ONE YOU PREFER.

CARTOONS	OR	LIVE ACTION
ART	OR	MATH
PLAN IT	OR	WING IT
BACKPACK	OR	SUITCASE
EARLY BIRD	OR	NIGHT OWL
SUNRISE	OR	SUNSET
DREAMER	OR	REALIST
ALWAYS EARLY	OR	ALWAYS LATE
VANILLA	OR	CHOCOLATE
TALK TO ALL ANIMALS	OR	SPEAK ALL LANGUAGES
BE INVISIBLE	OR	FLY
SOCKS	OR	BARE FEET
SUN	OR	MOON
ICE CREAM	OR	GELATO
HOT DOG	OR	HAMBURGER

Date:

Mother

WHAT'S ON YOUR MIND?

Date:

Daughter

WHAT'S ON YOUR MIND?

Date:

Mother

My Top 3 Favorites!

Top 3 Favorite Seasons

1.
2.
3.

Top 3 Favorite Restaurants

1.
2.
3.

My Top 3 Favorite Foods

1.
2.
3.

Date:

My Top 3 Favorites!

TOP 3 FAVORITE SEASONS

1.
2.
3.

TOP 3 FAVORITE RESTAURANTS

1.
2.
3.

MY TOP 3 FAVORITE FOODS

1.
2.
3.

Date:

Dear Younger Me,

Date:

Dear Older Me,

Date: _____

Mother

DOODLE WEATHER THINGS.

Date:

Doodle weather things.

Date:

Mother

My Favorite Things This Week

The best thing that happened this week:

....
....
....
....
....

My Favorite Products This Week:

....
....
....
....

My Favorite Everything Else This Week:

....
....
....
....
....
....
....

Date:

My Favorite Things This Week

 **Daughter**

The best thing that happened this week:

....
....
....
....
....

My Favorite Products This Week:

....
....
....
....
....

My Favorite Everything Else This Week:

....
....
....
....
....
....
....

_____
Date:

Mother

Would You Rather

Write your own would you rather questions for your daughter.

Would you rather ....
   Or
Would you rather ....

Would you rather ....
   Or
Would you rather ....

Would you rather ....
   Or
Would you rather ....

Would you rather ....
   Or
Would you rather ....

Would you rather ....
   Or
Would you rather ....

Would you rather ....
   Or
Would you rather ....

Date:

Would You Rather

Daughter

Write Your Own Would You Rather questions for your mother.

Would you rather ....
 Or
Would you rather ....

Would you rather ....
 Or
Would you rather ....

Would you rather ....
 Or
Would you rather ....

Would you rather ....
 Or
Would you rather ....

Would you rather ....
 Or
Would you rather ....

Would you rather ....
 Or
Would you rather ....

Date: _____

Mother

If you could have your own business selling anything in the world, real or fake, what would it be?

Date:

Daughter

If you could have your own business selling anything in the world, real or fake, what would it be?

Date:

Mother

My Top 3 UN Favorites!

My top 3 disliked candies
1.
2.
3.

My top 3 disliked animals
1.
2.
3.

My top 3 disliked Instruments
1.
2.
3.

Date:

My Top 3 UN Favorites!

My top 3 disliked candies
1.
2.
3.

My top 3 disliked animals
1.
2.
3.

My top 3 disliked Instruments
1.
2.
3.

Date: _____

Mother

Why don't you like those candies?

Why don't you like those animals?

Why don't you like those Instruments?

Date:

Daughter

Why don't you like those candies?

....
....
....
....
....
....
....

Why don't you like those animals?

....
....
....
....
....
....
....

Why don't you like those Instruments?

....
....
....
....
....
....
....

Date:

Mother

Ask Me 3 Questions:

Daughter's Question 1:

....
....

Mother's Answer:

....
....
....

Daughter's Question 2:

....
....

Mother's Answer:

....
....
....

Daughter's Question 3:

....
....

Mother"s Answer:

....
....
....

Date:

Ask Me 3 Questions: Daughter

Mother's Question 1:

Daughter's Answer:

Mother's Question 2:

Daughter's Answer:

Mother's Question 3:

Daughter's Answer:

Date:

Mother

DOODLE KIND WORDS ABOUT YOUR DAUGHTER.

Date:

DOODLE KIND WORDS ABOUT YOUR MOTHER.

Date:

Mother

What would you do if you were invisible?

Date:

What would you do if you were invisible?

Date:

Mother

My Favorite Things This Week

The Best Thing That Happened This Week:

....
....
....
....
....

My Favorite Products This Week:

....
....
....
....

My Favorite Everything Else This Week:

....
....
....
....
....
....

Date:

My Favorite Things This Week

 Daughter

The best thing that happened this week:

_____
_____
_____
_____
_____

My Favorite Products This Week:

_____
_____
_____
_____
_____

My Favorite Everything Else This Week:

_____
_____
_____
_____
_____
_____
_____

Date: _____

Mother

5 Quick Questions

What is the most unpleasant sounding word?

What is the best sounding word?

If you can have a mini version of any animal, what mini animal would you have?

What is your dream job?

What is you most treasured material item?

Date:

5 Quick Questions

What is the most unpleasant sounding word?

_____

What is the best sounding word?

_____

If you can have a mini version of any animal, what mini animal would you have?

_____

What is your dream job?

_____

What is you most treasured material item?

_____

Date: _____

Mother

WHAT'S ON YOUR MIND?

Date:

WHAT'S ON YOUR MIND?

Daughter

Date:

Mother

If your Daughter was a cartoon character, which one would she be and why?

Date:

If your Mother was a cartoon character, which one would she be and why?

Date:

Mother

My Favorite Things This Week

The best thing that happened this week:

....
....
....
....
....

My Favorite Products This Week:

....
....
....
....
....

My Favorite Everything Else This Week:

....
....
....
....
....
....
....

Date:

My Favorite Things This Week

The best thing that happened this week:

....
....
....
....
....

My Favorite Products This Week:

....
....
....
....
....

My Favorite Everything Else This Week:

....
....
....
....
....
....
....

Date: _____

Doodle food things.

Date: _____

DOODLE FOOD THINGS.

Date:

Mother

What was your favorite grade in school and why?

Date:

What has been your favorite grade in school and why?

Date:

Mother

My Top 3 UN Favorites!

My top 3 disliked cars

1.
2.
3.

My top 3 disliked celebrities

1.
2.
3.

My top 3 disliked flowers

1.
2.
3.

_____
Date:

Daughter

My Top 3 UN Favorites!

My top 3 disliked cars

1.
2.
3.

My top 3 disliked celebrities

1.
2.
3.

My top 3 disliked flowers

1.
2.
3.

Date: _____

Mother

Why don't you like those cars?

....
....
....
....
....
....
....
....

Why don't you like those celebrities?

....
....
....
....
....
....
....
....

Why don't you like those flowers?

....
....
....
....
....
....
....
....

_____
Date:

Daughter

Why don't you like those cars?

....
....
....
....
....
....
....

Why don't you like those celebrities?

....
....
....
....
....
....
....

Why don't you like those flowers?

....
....
....
....
....
....
....

Date:

Mother

My Favorite Things This Week

The best thing that happened this week:

....
....
....
....
....

My Favorite Products This Week:

....
....
....
....
....

My Favorite Everything Else This Week:

....
....
....
....
....
....
....

_____
Date:

My Favorite Things This Week

Daughter

The best thing that happened this week:

....
....
....
....
....

My Favorite Products This Week:

....
....
....
....
....

My Favorite Everything Else This Week:

....
....
....
....
....
....
....

_____
Date:

Mother

MY TOP 3 FAVORITES!

TOP 3 FAVORITE COLORS

1.
2.
3.

TOP 3 FAVORITE SHAPES

1.
2.
3.

MY TOP 3 FAVORITE FRUITS

1.
2.
3.

Date:

My Top 3 Favorites!

Daughter

top 3 favorite Colors

1.
2.
3.

top 3 Favorite Shapes

1.
2.
3.

My top 3 Favorite Fruits

1.
2.
3.

Date: _____

Mother

Circle the one you prefer.

1. Do you like going to school? YES NO

2. Do you want to make a time capsule? YES NO

3. Do you believe in aliens? YES NO

4. Do you fall asleep easily? YES NO

5. Do you like doing DIY projects? YES NO

6. Do you believe in love at first sight? YES NO

7. Do you like comic books? YES NO

8. Do you like cooking? YES NO

9. Have you ever been afraid of the dark? YES NO

10. Would you ever skydive? YES NO

_____
Date:

CIRCLE THE ONE YOU PREFER.

1. Do you like going to school? YES NO

2. Do you want to make a time capsule? YES NO

3. Do you believe in aliens? YES NO

4. Do you fall asleep easily? YES NO

5. Do you like doing DIY projects? YES NO

6. Do you believe in love at first sight? YES NO

7. Do you like comic books? YES NO

8. Do you like cooking? YES NO

9. Have you ever been afraid of the dark? YES NO

10. Would you ever skydive? YES NO

Date:

Mother

Write a love letter to your Daughter.

Date:

Daughter

Write a love letter to your Mother.

Date:

www.ingramcontent.com/pod-product-compliance
Lightning Source LLC
Chambersburg PA
CBHW081138010526
44110CB00061B/2519